**Editions THILL s.a. Bruxelles**

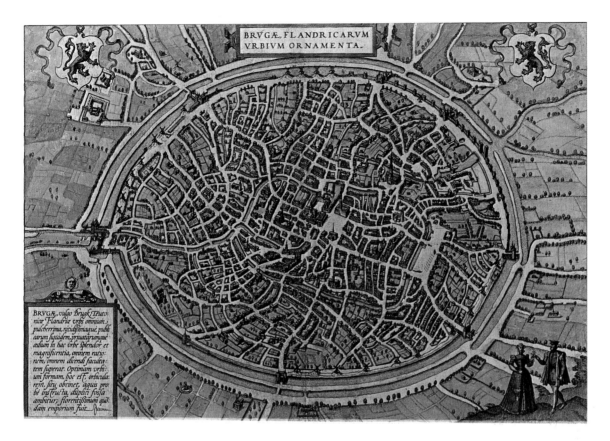

Between the 7th and 9th century a small settlement was established on the banks of the «Zwin». The first inhabitants who sought refuge there named it Bryggia. The town that was to become an important commercial centre, thanks to its harbour, grew up around the «Burg» fortress, built by the Counts of Flanders. Such was the importance of Bruges that the Counts took up permanent residence and minted their own coinage.

A port of international standing in the 13th century, Bruges fell into economic decline two centuries later due to silting up of the «Zwin»; the city's role was the taken over by Antwerp.

Nevertheless, Bruges soon regained its former splendour as the seat of the Dukes of Burgundy. It grew into a city of great splendour, a city without rival as centre for the arts. The ancient architecture of Bruges makes an essential contribution to the artistic patrimony of Europe. The paintings by Flemish Primitives housed in its museums are charged with emotion for the visitor. The 15th century school of painting at Bruges, enjoying the patronage of the Dukes of Burgundy, numbered among its artists masters of genius, such as Jan Van Eyck, painter to the court Philip the Good, Petrus Christus, Hugo van der Goes, Gerard David, Hans Memlinc, Roger van der Weyden, Dirk Bouts and many others... the Renaissance period is represented by Lancelot Blondeel and Pieter Pourbus.

From the 14th century onwards a tradition in wrought iron work, tapestry weaving and embroidery evolved at Bruges; its lace making, moreover, has been world famous since the Middle Ages. At the beginning of this century the city was provided with an outlet to the sea once more by the construction of the Zeebruges canal. In the seventies, a port for ocean-going ships was built.

Thus, the town that emerged from the sea, from which it gained its well-being, has once more, thanks to the sea, achieved the prosperity necessary for social and economic growth and the means to safeguard its inestimable patrimony. The presence of water in every corner of the city is one of the great charms of Bruges.

The **Belfry and Market Hall** were built in c. 1240 and completed with a wooden tower. The building was used by town magistrates as an assembly hall. In 1280 the tower was destroyed by fire, together with the Records Office and the Treasury. The new tower, built from stone, was completed in c. 1300. The complex formed by the two buildings is 84 m long and 45 m wide. The «**Grand Place**» (Main Square) has been the hub of city life for centuries. The foundations of economic, political and social life were laid here: knights defended their titles, fishmongers put up their stalls, politics and the Flemish textile industry were discussed and the population fought for its civil rights. The gibbet, the guillotine, as well as the «Tree of Liberty» were all erected on the «Grand Place».

Baldwin III, Count of Flanders, is widely believed to have founded the weekly market held on Saturdays here.

5

Between the 14th and 18th century the authorities gave public proclamation to the laws and regulations governing the market from the balcony above the entrance to the Belfry. The statue of Our Lady to be seen above the balcony, like the other 600 statues of the Virgin scattered around the city, is garlanded in the month of May.

The medallion bears the coat of arms of the Dynasty. The small corner towers on the second storey date from the 14th century. The open-air octagonal gallery was built at the end of the 15th century and from here, after climbing the 366 steps of the 83 m high tower, the view out over the Flemish countryside may be admired.

The carillon of the Belfry in Bruges is renowned for its range: from the keyboard the bell-ringer commands a peal of 47 bells (with an overall weight of 27,000 kg.) that ring out charming melodies.

The buildings standing on the eastern side of the «Grand-Place» are the **Gouvernement Provincial**(the seat of provincial administration) and the Post Office. Both are in the Gothic style; their foundations were laid in 1887.

A number of buildings with corbie-stepped gables also flank the «Grand-Place». These were originally guildhalls.

The remarkable 15th century Bruges-style house «**Maison Bouchoute**» stands on the corner of Saint-Amand street. Another, equally well-known adornment to the square is the **Craenenburg house** in which Maximilian of Austria was held prisoner by town rebels in 1488.

Centrally placed on the main square are the bronze and stone statues portraying the butcher **Jan Breydel** and the weaver **Pieter de Coninck,** both of whom fought bravely in the battle for indipendence from France in 1302.

The monument to these popular Flemish heroes was put up in 1887 by P. de Vigne and L. de la Censerie. The crucial moments of the battle are illustrated on the base of the monument.

**Breydel street,** location of the civic records office, brings us face to face with the Baroque building of the **Prévôté**, once the seat of provosts of the no longer extant S. Donation chatedral.

Beetwen 1089 and 1559 all church dignitaries were rightful knights of Flanders. In 1559 Bruges was made a bishopric and the title of provost was accorded to the first bishop.

The lower chapel of the **Basilican Church of the Holy Blood** was built in the 12th century. It was commissioned by Count Thierry of Alsace to house the relics of St Basil the Great. The chapel, the oldest in the city, still bears the saint's name.

Above the side entrance in the original wall, the 12th century «Tympanum», the most ancient carving surviving in Bruges. It represents the baptism of St Basil in the waters of the Jordan, celebrated, according to legend, by Maximilian, Bishop of Jerusalem. A pigeon appears in the sky.

— A work of unknown origin. It might be the retable of a way-side altar of the period.

The **Madonna** or Virgin and Child, carved by a French sculptor in c. 1300, a period of stylistic transition between Romanesque and Gothic. It was placed in its present location at a later date.

«**Ecce Homo**», a sacred theme carved in pinewood by D'Hondt of Bruges in c. 1900. Popularly known as «Jesus on the cold stone» or «Jesus on a small wooden plinth», the paint surface of the knees has been worn away by the devout fingers of the faithful.

The «**Piétà**» carved by De Wispelaere of Bruges so as to allow drapes to be changed, portrays the Mother of God with the lifeless body of Jesus across her knees. The people of Bruges revere the work as «The God of Succour».

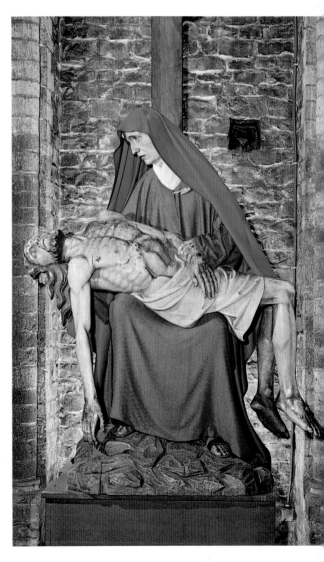

In the 12th century a second chapel was built above the extant Romanesque lower chapel, in the same style. Twice destroyed (in the 16th century and almost entirely in 1795 during the French Revolution), it was rebuilt, on the second occasion in 1829, in the Neo-Gothic style.

Pope Pius XI accorded the building the status of Basilica on 13 April 1923.

The white marble altar in the Rococo style was built to a design by Hendrik Pulinx in 1715. It was transferred here from the chapel of the deputy burgomasters in the «Brugse Vrije» in 1824, serving initially as the high altar. The silver tabernacle by the Bruges silversmith Reylandt was installed in 1773, followed by the silver cross on 3 May 1781. The great silver candlesticks date from 1688. At the foot of the cross a white marble lamb is to be remarked, surrounded by the symbols of the four evangelists.

Besides the altar to be seen in the Chapel of the Cross, on Fridays throughout the year the relic itself is exhibited to the faithful. The throne on which it is placed was designed by W. Brangwyn. The silver lamp placed before the throne dates from 1611 and was donated by the archduchess Isabella.

The upper chapel housing the relic is reached by the «de Steeghere» monumental stairway, dating from 1529-1533. The original Romanesque character of the chapel is somewhat obscured by later interventions in the Gothic style. The Gothic style silver lamp dates from 1740 and the alabaster panel of the 'Last Supper' inset in the new altar, from 1556.

According to tradition, the relic of the Holy Blood was donated to Thierry of Alsace, Count of Flanders, founder of the chapel of St Basil, by Fucher, Patriarch of Jerusalem and Baldwin III, king of the city, and brother-in-law to Thierry, on Christmas Day 1148. On his return to Bruges, the count donated the relic to the town.

The crystal sheath with its small gold crowns holds the rock crystal container, the neck of which is bound with fine gold wire and its stopper sealed with red wax. The vessel, of Constantinople provenance, dates from the 11th or 12th century. It is still intact today, with its content of sheep's wool impregnated with blood, and reliable evidence exists to confirm its presence in the city in 1250.

The reliquary is supported by angels in gilded copper and silver. When celebrations take place it is placed on the high altar.

The **Stained Glass Windows** are replicas of the originals, today in the Victoria and Albert Museum in London. They portray:
— Mary of Burgundy (who fell from her horse and died a few days later, in 1482) and her husband, Maximilian I, Emperor of Germany.
— Her grand parents, Philip the Good, Count of Flanders, Duke of Burgundy, founder of the Order of the Golden Fleece, and Isabella of Portugal, whom he married in Bruges in 1430.
— Her parents, Charles the Bold and his second wife, Isabella of Aragon.
- Her son, Philip the Fair, born in Bruges, and Joan of Aragon.
- Her grandson, Charles V, Emperor of the Holy Roman Empire and Isabella of Portugal.

The gold and silver reliquary, protecting the relic during processions, is displayed in the museum. It was created by the goldsmith Jan Crabbe of Bruges in 1617. The work is richly decorated with gold statuettes, precious stones and cameos. The casket bears the coats of arms of the counts of Flanders, the archdukes, Thierry of Alsace, and the city of Bruges. The reliquary is surmounted by a crown thought to have belonged to Mary of Burgundy.

The small silver reliquary was donated by the archdukes Albert and Isabella in 1612. In 1716 it was given a chased silver lid; a garland of flowers, gold roses inset with topazes, was added in 1890.

The gilded silver chalice with the words «Passibus Aequis 1652» engraved on the base and «Kelk van de H.H. Basilius gezeid van den H. Bloed» (St Basil's or Holy Blood chalice) on the side, is still used in the course of ceremonies today.

The Noble Brotherhood of the Holy Blood (De Edele Broederschap van het Heling Bloed), an association of 30 prominent citizens responsible for organizing the **Procession of the Holy Blood,** was already in existence in 1405. The procession, a pageant illustrating themes from the Gospels, takes place on Ascension Day each year.

The former **Records Office** was built in the Flemish Renaissance style. The carved stonework was replaced after destruction in 1792. The bronze statues represent Moses the Law Giver, Aaron the High Priest, and Justice. Initially the building housed the town archives. After the French Revolution it became a police station and since 1883 it has housed the Magistrates' Court.

The Gothic **Town Hall**, the oldest extant in Flanders, was built in 1376. It was to become a model for town halls in other cities. The façade has six pointed arch windows and 48 aedicules to house statues. The original statues of biblical figures and Flemish princes were destroyed in 1712. The counts took an oath of fidelity to the civic authorities on the main balcony of the building.

The first assembly of the States General took place in the Town Hall in 1464. Both interior and exterior have since been remodelled. One of the ground-floor rooms is hung with paintings portraying figures and events of historical importance:
—the «Deat of Charles the Bold».
—«The Fatal Fall of Mary of Burgundy».
A monumental stairway leads up to the first floor with its famous **Gothic or Council Chamber**, originally two separate rooms. The chamber today is enhanced by its ornate, gilded ceiling. Much is to be admired here: mural paintings by the brothers Albert and Julien De Vriendt (1895) illustrating crucial moments in the history of Bruges; the Neo-Gothic chimney-piece by de Wispelaere; the brass statues of S. Donation, patron saint of the city and Louis van Maele, Count of Flanders, two masterpieces by J. Anthone.

The **Law Courts**, in the classical style, stand on the site of the 15th-16th century 'Brugse Vrije' palace, the only extant remains of which may be seen in the handsome façade overlooking the canal, and the renowned Chamber of the Deputy Burgomasters.

Between 1528 and 1581 the then Chamber of the Deputy Burgomasters in the «Vrije» was enriched by a now famous chimney-piece in the Renaissance style. The chimney-piece proper is of black marble, inset with four carved panels of white marble illustrating the Legend of the Chaste Susannah.
The upper area in oak pays homage to the Emperor Charles V, with carvings of him as Count of Flanders, flanked by his grandparents, and the coats of arms of his ancestors. The emperor's throne is decorated with portaits of members of the royal houses of Spain and Austria and a painting by G. de Thilbrugge evoking a Vrije tribunal session.

**The «Brug»** might be called the Acropolis of Bruges. A fortress was built here for Count Baldwin I, fighting off the Norman threat to the State of his father-in-law, Charles the Bald, King of France. Administrative buildings and sanctuaries were put up later, and today, in what is virtually an open-air museum, nine centuries of architecture may be admired.

**«Blinde Ezel»** (Blind Donkey), the street running alongside the town hall, gains its picturesque name from that of an old inn. On the right-hand side of the entrance there is a fine Baroque doorway; set into the wall on the left side, one of the locks of the four gates that once sealed off Brug Square.

The **«Groenerei»**, one of the most picturesque corners of Bruges, is set amidst old houses and trees overlooking the quiet canals.

To be seen on the **«Huidevettersplaats»** (Tanners' Square), the ancient tanning house (1630 - 1716), today housing an exhibition of Modern Applied Arts and Creative Crafts.

The **«Rozenhoedkaai»** is a great attraction for painters and photographers.

A patrician residence standing where the **Bridge of S. Jan Nepomuc** adjoins the «Wollestraat» bears a commemorative plaque with lines by Guido Gezelle.

The centre of the bridge holds the statue of the Bruges — born saint, Johannes Nepomucenus, Archbishop of Prague, whose martyred body was thrown into the Moldau in 1393.

The **«Dijver»** offers a delightful place for a stroll between houses and trees reflected in the quiet waters of the canal. An antiques market is held here at week-ends.

A 13th century gateway provides access to the «**Groeninge**» Museum, the municipal museum of fine arts, built on the site of a former Augustine monastery in 1930. It houses a most comprehensive collection of Flemish painting, ancient and modern.

School of Roger van der Weiden:
«Mater Dolorosa».

Jan Van Eyck (1390-1441):
The Madonna with the canon Georges van der
Paele, S. Donation and St George.

Gerard David (1460-1523): «The Baptism of Christ». P.
Breughel (1554-1638): «Payment of the Tithe».

Pieter Pourbus (1524-1584):
«Potrait of Jean Fernaguut».

OPVS PETRI
POVRBVS

**The «Gruuthuse» Museum** was originally the seat of the Lords of Gruuthuse (15th century) The best known member of this Bruges patrician family was Lodewijk van Gruuthuse Knight of the Golden Fleece. His motto «Plus est en vous» (There is More in You) is to be encountered throughout the building. In 1692, the mansion was a pawnbroker's shop. After restoration work between 1883 and 1898 it became the seat of the Bruges Society of Antiquities, and, since 1955, houses the Museum of Antiquities and Fine Arts.

This 15th century sculpture of a Herald Angel was probably part of a Brabantine Annunciation.
A solid silver chalice, the work of Antoine Kerckof, Bruges (1658-1660) .

◁ Tapestry «The Triumph of Alexander the Great» (16th century). A general view of the Great Hall.

The interior court of the patrician residence is used for «Sound and Light» displays on summer evenings. An old wrought-iron sign hangs from the wooden façade above the entry gate.

On the other side of the St Boniface bridge stands the chapel linking the Gruuthuse mansion with the chancel of the Church of Our Lady.

The **Church of Our Lady** began life in the 9th century as a modest chapel beyond the canal boundaries of the town. As its prestige grew it was replaced by a Romanesque building. By the 12th century the inhabitants of Bruges had astutely pushed out their town boundaries by deviating the course of canal waters and

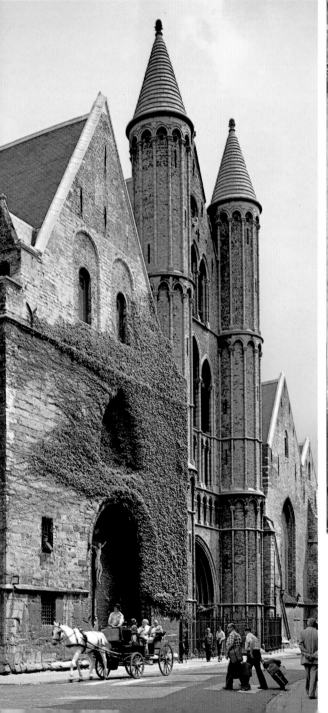

the church stood at the heart of the town. This unique Gothic monument dates from the 13th century. It is built almost entirely of brick and has undergone re-modelling several times over the centuries. The 122 m high Great Tower is the tallest brick tower in the Netherlands.

The central nave reveals the different phases of building this five-aisle church. The 30 coats of arms above the stalls belong to the knights present at the second Chapter of the Golden Fleece, held in the church in 1468. The chancel is partitioned off by a wrought-iron grille, and a triumphal crucifix (1594) hangs over the rood loft (1722). The statues of the apostles and the great candelabrum date from 1618. The carved oak pulpit (1743) was carried out to a design by Jan-Antoon Gaeremyn.

Despite the loss of many treasures the Church of Our Lady is still undeniably rich in works of art: a painting of **Our Lady of the Seven Sorrows** dating from between 1518 and 1535, by a Bruges artist, A. Isenbrandt.

A handsome work in Carrara marble, carved by Michelangelo at the beginning of the 14th century, «Our Lady and the Child Jesus» was bought by the Bruges merchant J. Moscroen in 1506 and donated to the church. It is one of the few works by the master to be found outside Italy.

The monstrance by the goldsmith Jean Beaucourt (1725) was donated by Marie-Madeleine van Westervelde, widow of François van Beversluys, collector-in-chief of the «Franc de Bruges». The central motif is a crown set with splendid diamonds, the gold rays wreathed in vine branches bearing bunches of seed-pearl grapes.

The **Mount of Calvary**, a great tryptych by Bernard van Orley, was commissioned by Margaret of Austria to commemorate her husband. It was donated to the church unfinished, and completed by Marcus Gerard in 1561.

**The mausoleum of Mary of Burgundy** in the Gothic style, was commissioned from J. Borman by Philip the Fair. It was cast in bronze by R. van Thienen and gilded by P. de Beckere (1498-1502). At 19 years of age, Mary of Burgundy married the irascible Maximilian of Austria. Her accidental death at the age of 25 took place while out hunting with a falcon.

The Renaissance style **mausoleum of Charles the Bold**, father of Mary of Burgundy, was commissioned by Philip III and modelled on that of his sister. The work in bronze is by J. Jonghelink and the stone carving by J. Aerts and J. De Smet. Charles the Bold died on the battlefield at Nancy in 1477. In 1550 the emperor Charles V had his great-grand father's mortal remains transported to Bruges. Besides the recumbent statues, the enamelled coats of arms and the family tree of the dynasty are also worthy of attention.

**St John's Hospital** is one of the oldest in Europe. It was already standing in the 12th century, when it was also used as a rest-house for travellers. One room, a hospital ward in the 13th century, today houses the Memlinc museum, in which masterpieces by the German-born Hans Memlinc, who died in Bruges in 1494, are reverently displayed.

The porch on the Romanesque-style central façade, with restoration work on the arch. The two pointed arches of the tympanum are inset with carvings of the Death of Mary and the Assumption of the Virgin. The medallion represents the Coronation of the Mother of God.

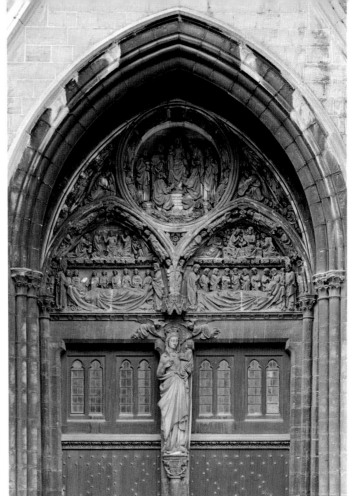

The convent displays all manner of furniture. The old hospital pharmacy with its Renaissance furnishings and ancient instruments is worth a visit.

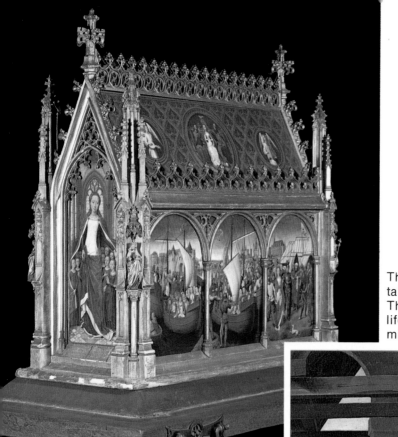

The wooden **reliquary of St Ursula** takes the form of a Gothic chapel. The side panels portray episodes in the life of the saint. This is a masterpiece of miniature painting.

**The Visit of the Three Wise Men.**

50

**Page 51**
**The Mystic Marriage of St Catherine.** The Child Jesus, seated in Our Lady's lap, places the ring on St Catherine's finger.

The **«Minnewater»** (Lake of Love), as poetic as its legend is a source of inspiration for lovers and dreamers.

Since 1488 — according to an old legend — swans have been shown special favours here. Rebel citizens of Bruges holding the noble archduke Maximilian of Austria prisoner, condemned to death his servant Pieter Lanchais. The archduke consented to meet rebel demands, but, in reprisal for the death of his faithful servant condemned the citizens of Bruges to take care of the swans until the end of time. White swans belong to the city and are marked on the beak with the capital letter B and the date of birth.

**The "Sashuis"** ("Sluice-gate") is an elegant building dating from the XVIth century.

**The Beguinage** was founded in 1245 by Margaret of Costantinople, Countess of Flanders. It offers a perfect setting for leisurely strolls in green surroundings. Under the guidance of an unmarried noblewoman, a «Grande Demoiselle», the beguines led a life of prayer and washed wool for weavers in the canal waters alongside the beguinage. The «princely beguinage», as it was called after the French king Philip the Fair divested Bruges magistrates of their jurisdiction, was abandoned by the beguines in 1928.

The religious atmosphere was restored in 1930 by the setting up of a community of Benedictine nuns here, that adopted the beguines' style of dress.

The Convent of Benedictine nuns, daughters off the Church.

**The Convent** comprises a number of houses, extending from the small chapel on the west side to the big chapel on the south.

The convent building proper, where the nuns live, is hidden from view behind the old façades.

The 14th century **Beguinage Church** is dedicated to St Elizabeth, first patron of the beguinage. The Louis XVI and XVII furnishings are authentic. St Elizabeth is portrayed in a painting by J. Van Oost above the high altar. Facing the church, two adjoining upper fronts are to be seen. These belong to guest rooms set apart by the Benedictine order so that convent guests may enjoy the meditative atmosphere to the full.

**The Beguine's House** is open to visitor. It is a small 17th century building, entirely unchanged since it was built, its layout comprising a living room, a kitchen, a bedroom with old furniture, a beguine's chest, a provision cupboard, a linen press used by the beguines to keep their fine tuckers neat, lace curtains, and a small but very precious collection of old laces. Lastly, a small garden with a tiny lawn and a well in the courtyard.

«WHAT ENHANCES THE DESERT IS THE PRESENCE SOMEWHERE OF A WELL. . . »

Skiful lace-makers can be observed on the **Walplaats** in the summertime.

**The Bishop's Palace,** originally a patrician residence, was rebuilt in the Renaissance style in 1549. The bishops of Bruges have lived here since 1835.

The **Church of S. Sauveur** is thought to have been conceived by St Eligius, Bishop of Noyon, in c. 640. It was the first parish church of Bruges and underwent remodelling on several occasions before the 13th century when the rich bourgeoisie built a new church in the Gothic style. This was begun in 1280 and completed in 1350. The building has survived four fires and the effects of the French Revolution. After the church of S. Donation was demolished and reform of the archduchy took place, it was elevated to cathedral status.

The Neo-Romanesque tower was completed in the 19th century. The high altar dates from 1642 and was designed by J. Cocx. Statues of the three patron saints of the church, S. Sauveur, S. Donation, and St Eligius, stand above the altar. The pulpit supported on eagle's legs dates from 1605.

The rood loft and organ-case (end of the 17th to beginning of the 18th century) stand at the back of the church. At the centre, God the Father, carved in white marble by A. Quellin the Younger in 1682. The Louis XVI pulpit is the work of H. Pulicx. The statue of St Eligius bearing the church plans was carved by L. Taminne in 1780. The choir stalls, one of the major adornments of the church, date from 1430 and carry the coats of arms evoking the 13th Chapter of the Golden Fleece, held in the church in 1478. The tapestries were commissioned by the bishop Van Susteren in 1731 and woven in Brussels by Van der Borght. The great door was built of sheet copper and cast in 1708 by W. Somers.

The church was adorned with masterpieces of art transferred here from other churches and convents. The museum houses several remarkable works:

— a tryptych by Dirk Bouts «The torture of St Hippolytus» (1470-1474)

— the chapter room contains embroidered cloths portraying the Madonna flanked by the Four Doctors of the Church, and a Tryptych of the «Last Supper» by P. Pourbus (1599).

**Simon Stevin,** mathematician, philosopher and architect, was the greatest mind Bruges has known. He was born here in 1548 and died at The Hague in 1620.

Many inventions are owed to him. He travelled throughout Europe and was the tutor of Prince Maurice of Nassau. The statue, put up by E. Simonisin 1847, stands at the centre of the square bearing his name.

**Stock Exchange Square** (La Place de la Bourse) owes its name to a certain patrician merchant, Van de Beurse, who became established here in the 13th century. Foreign merchants came to keep a check on the market. International trade was carried on in the open air and Bruges became a model for European stock exchanges, a centre for bankers and financiers from Venice, Florence, Lucca and Genoa. The splendid mansions of foreign nationals, in which merchants displayed their wares and set up their consulates, evolved in this way. The present-day façade of the «Huis ter Beurse» dates from the 15th century.

The **Church of St James** was built without a nave in c. 1240. It was enlarged in the 15th century, thanks to donations from the dukes of Burgundy and from rich merchants. The Gothic church was compelled to yield up a great part of its artistic patrimony to the iconoclasts in 1580. Restoration in the Baroque style took two centuries. The interior is very harmonious and well-endowed with art treasures.

**Jan Van Eyck** was born in the Meuse region and died in Bruges in 1492. He was an innovator in the field of painting technique and the father of the Flemish school of painting. The bronze statue (1878) is the work of the Bruges sculptor Henri Pickery.

The «**Burghers'Lodge**» is an original building dating from the 15th century, albeit partially rebuilt after fire in 1755. It was a meeting place for the most eminent citizens of Bruges. The most renowned of these were honoured with a statue: among them the legendary bear, the oldest inhabitant of Bruges, who also appears in the city's coat of arms. The lodge houses state archives, together with ecclesiastic and municipal documents dating back to the 11th century.

**The City Library** is housed in the old «Tonlieu» building. It numbers some 100,000 books and 600 manuscripts from the old Abbey of the Dunes.
The coat of arms of the rulers of Luxembourg is framed above the entrance. Duties on goods transported to market in earlier times had to be paid at this building. The slim façade on its left belonged to the porters' guild.

The statue of **Hans Memlinc** was erected by H. Pickery in 1871. Renowned painter of pensive Madonnas, portraits and altarpieces, Memlinc was born in Germany but early in life settled in Bruges, where he died 11 August 1494. He is known as the Flemish Fra Angelico.

**Our Lady of the Pottery,** built in 1276 as a women's hospital with a nursing staff of Augustine nuns, took its name from a potters' chapel formerly on the site. The building has a private chapel and a well-endowed museum.

**The Guild of the Archers of St Sebastian** has held the building since 1573. According to tradition, the archers took part in the crusades and since that time the guild escutcheon incorporates the coat of arms of the city of Jerusalem. In the Middle Ages the archers formed part of the town militia and by the 14th century had become a powerful association. Today the guild performs a purely recreational function. Charles II, who became an honorary member of the guild during his three years of exile here, took his royal pleasures in this building. Important documents are preserved in the records office and in the king's chamber.

Three windmills are still standing in an idyllic setting on the green hills of the «**Kruisvest**». Originally, there were 27 identical mills encircling the town, visible from the ramparts. The miller shows visitors round the St John's windmill, still storing flour. Guido Gezelle used to visit this mill when it was still in effective use, to listen to the millers' tales.

Guido Gezelle, the greatest Flemish poet of lyrical and historical themes, was born lst May 1830 and died 27 November 1899. His house has been kept as a museum since 1926. Manuscripts, paintings, translations and the personal possessions of the priest-poet are on display. The statue of this much-loved son of Bruges stands beneath a shady cedar tree behind his house.

**The Jerusalem Church** is one of the rare places in Belgium that has kept its original style and remained in private hands. During the 14th century a noble Genoese family built the chapel, which was completed in 1470. It is said to be inspired by the Church of the Holy Sepulchre in Jerusalem. The interior has a single nave and a raised chancel. The funerary monument of the Anselm Adornes-Vander Banck couple stands at the centre of the church.

The present-day **Church of St Anne** was consecrated in 1624. It replaced an earlier Gothic church, destroyed by vandals in 1581. The church resembles its patron saint: modest outwardly and richly endowed within. The Baroque style gives the interior a very special atmosphere. The most remarkable furnishing is the marble rood loft by H. van Mildert (1626 - 1628). The landescapes by J. Garemijn and the statue of St Anne date from the 15th century. The Bruges poet Guido Gezelle was baptized here.

**The Church of St Walburga** was built between 1629 and 1642 by Bruges-born P. Huyssens of the Jesuit order. Originally the church was attached to the Jesuit convent and dedicated to St Francis Xavier, whose statue may be seen in a niche above the entrance. At the time of the French Revolution it was deconsecrated and rededicated to Reason. In 1802 it was reconsecrated. It houses precious furnishings, such as the pulpit (1667-1669) by A. Quellin the Younger, the marble communion table and the high altar, carved by H. Verbruggen.

Only four of the original seven town gates in the encircling walls survive intact: the Donkey Gate, the Marshal's Gate, the Gate of the Holy Cross and the Ghent Gate.

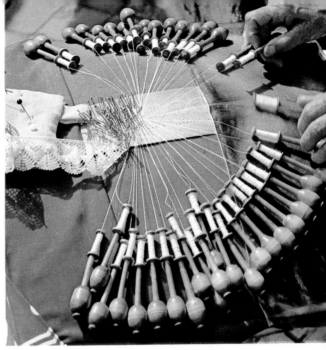

The most typical textile craft of Bruges is undoubtedly lace-making, its product known throughout Europe until the 17th century as «Flanders Lace». The most sought after Bruges lace is created with the «sorciere» stitch, calling for from between 300 and 700 bobbins.

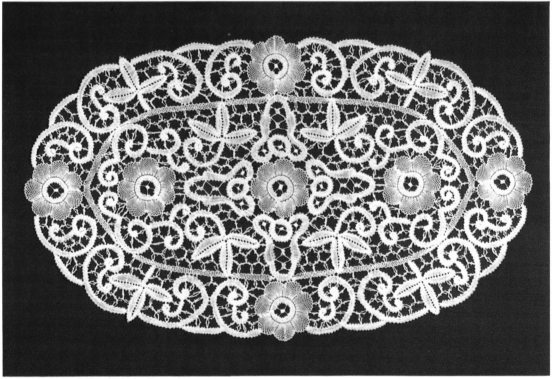

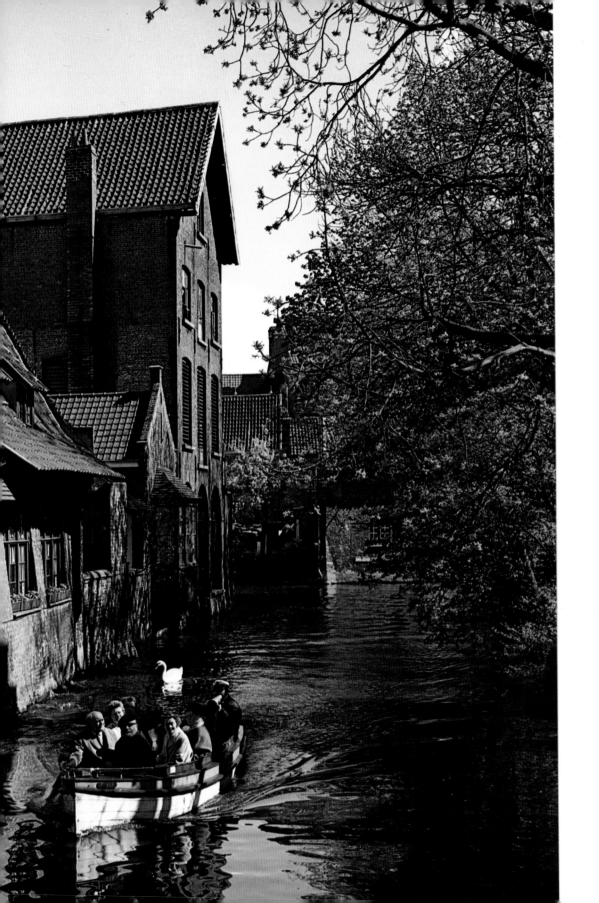

Horse-drawn cabs and small boats offer the only chance of discovering picturesque corners of an unusual district of the city. One might liken the experience to a fairy tale beginning: «Once upon a time...»

The little bridges, the canals and their swans, lend Bruges that romantic atmosphere one would like to capture with one's pen, on canvas, or with the camera. A delightful, charming, captivating town, where one may always discover new, hidden treasures.

Bruges, a lively town in which past and present blend together wonderfully well: one that also induces peace of mind. Its hospitality from the times of medieval merchants and 15th century artists to the present age of business men and tourists, is renowned throughout the world.

# INDEX